Song Of
SOLOMON

GOD'S LOVE SONG FOR ISRAEL

Study outlines on the greatest song of history

Randy White

Copyright © 2019 Randy White
Cover and Illustration: Leonardo Costa
Cover and Illustrations © 2019 DispensationalPublishing House, Inc.

All rights reserved. This book or any portion thereof may not be reproduced or used in any manner whatsoever without the express written permission of the publisher except for the use of brief quotations in a book review.

Scriptures quoted as KJV are taken from the KING JAMES VERSION (KJV).

Printed in the United States of America
First Edition, First Printing, 2019
ISBN: 978-1-945774-35-5

Dispensational Publishing House, Inc.
220 Paseo del Pueblo Norte
Taos, NM 87571

www.dispensationalpublishing.com

DISPENSATIONAL
QuickPRINT

This is a DPH Quick Print book. Our QuickPrint process allows us to get books to the market at a much quicker pace and lower cost than the full book publishing process. If you discover errors in this book, please contact the publisher so that these errors may be fully removed in future editions.

Ordering Information: Quantity sales. Special discounts are available on quantity purchases by churches, associations, and others. For details, contact the publisher at the address above.

Orders by U.S. trade bookstores and wholesalers. Please contact the publisher:
Tel: (844) 321-4202

1 2 3 4 5 6 7 8 9 10

Dedicated to my Jewish friends located around the world. You have helped my faith tremendously, taught me marvelous insights in theology, and give me the assurance that the promises of G-d to Abraham are being fulfilled and will be fully delivered.

Table of Contents

Preface 1
Introduction to Song of Solomon 3
Song of Solomon 1:1-17 9
Song of Solomon 2:1-17 17
Song of Solomon 3:1-11 23
Song of Solomon 4:1-5:1 27
Song of Solomon 5:2-16 33
Song of Solomon 6:1-13 39
Song of Solomon 6:13-7:13 45
Song of Solomon 8:1-14 51

PREFACE

The Song of Solomon is a Song of Songs! It is a love story, no doubt. It is historical, no doubt. But everyone agrees it is *so much more!*

The question of the ages has been, *"What is the much more?"* Is it a song about love, marriage, and sex? Many pastors have taught it so, and brought in great crowds (and sold many volumes of books) by making it some kind of God-ordained sex manual. Or maybe it is a love song between God and the church, which has been known as "the bride of Christ" since the earliest days of the Catholic church, and into the Protestant Reformation, and continuing to these days of evangelicalism. I don't take this approach because I don't think the text of the song, nor full Biblical text, allows it.

I believe this is a prophetic song about the relationship between God and Israel. These study notes are an attempt to show how wonderfully the Song of Solomon fits with the theology of the Hebrew Scriptures.

These notes are a study guide. You can use them in your own verse-by-verse study. Use them as a commentary, as a sounding board, as a means of questioning the assumptions (yours and mine). Use them in personal study or group study. However you use them, I pray that you find spiritual growth and Biblical understanding as you study God's Word, especially as given in the Song of Solomon.

Should you desire, the original video recordings of these sessions are available at www.RandyWhiteMinistries.org. This website contains thousands of hours of verse-by-verse exegetical Bible teaching from a dispensational perspective. Perhaps you would like to join us for our regular Thursday night online Bible study, or for our daily "Ask the Theologian" broadcasts, or just to find this Song of Solomon study archived, along with so much more.

May God bless you as you *rightly divide the word of truth*.

In His Grace;

Randy White

Taos, NM

INTRODUCTION TO SONG OF SOLOMON

The Major Issue: an Interpretive Grid

- Option 1: The book is to be interpreted literally as a marriage manual.
- Option 2: The book is a historic love story to be interpreted allegorically.
  - As the love between Christ and the church.
  - As the love between Christ and the Christian.
  - As the love between God and Israel.

My Position and Defense

- I believe that the book is a historic love story that shows God's love for Israel.
- Defense of this position:
  - Why I don't take a literal interpretation:

- Until modern times, such an interpretation was unheard of.
- Mankind doesn't need a Biblical revelation for effective sex.
- Why I don't accept the view that says the book is an allegory concerning Christ's love for the church or the Christian:
  - This is not the story of the love of an existing relationship; it is the story of the enticement of a love that doesn't exist.
  - It is the *renewed love* of the remnant that is the subject of the book.
  - When the remnant of Israel falls in love with Christ, He will then be fully known as her King.

The Key Verse

▶ Song of Solomon 8:1 is the key verse to understanding the song.

- **O that thou *wert* as my brother, that sucked the breasts of my mother! *When* I should find thee without, I would kiss thee; Yea, I should not be despised** (Song. 8:1).

▶ This verse shares the desire that Christ the Messiah has for Israel: to be in a very natural and very open relationship that would never be questioned.

- The King is going to express His love until His goal is reached and it can be said, "**I am my beloved's, and my beloved is mine**" (Song. 6:3).

Understanding Chapter 1

▶ Chapter 1 gives the overview and the end of the matter, and in later chapters, the detail will be given.

- Like the prophecy of the Psalms, the *revelation* is given in early chapters, followed by the description of the *remnant*.
- Love-talk in Chapter 1:
  - The loved remnant (the woman) speaks of the qualities of her Beloved King, and she does so openly and proudly.
  - The King (the man) speaks reassuringly of his delight in the woman.
- We notice that the woman in the song will be much more variable in her love and needy of the King's reassurance.

The Jewish Interpretation

- The Jewish Targum (commentary) teaches that there are 10 songs in the Bible:
  - The song of Adam on the Sabbath – Psalm 92
  - The song of Moses at the parting of the sea – Exodus 15
  - The song of Israel – Numbers 21:17
  - The song of Moses at his pending death – Deuteronomy 32
  - The song of Joshua when the sun stood still – Joshua 10:12
  - The song of Deborah and Barak on the defeat of Sisera – Judges 5:1
  - The song of Hannah when praying for a son – 1 Samuel 2:1
  - The song of David when celebrating his blessings – 2 Samuel 22:1
  - The song of Solomon – the entire book
  - The song of the future redeemed – Isaiah 30:29

- The Targum also teaches that the history of Israel is embedded in chapter 1:
    - Verse 4 – The desire of the righteous to follow the *shekinah* glory
    - Verse 5 – The embarrassment over the creation of the golden calf, which the sages said caused the creators to be covered in soot and ash.
    - Verse 6 – The assembly of Israel addresses the assembly of nations, saying that they are darker than the other nations because they followed the pagan practices of the other nations. In this sense, "black" is not a reference to skin color but to sin.
    - Verse 7 – This is the plea of Moses, according to the Jewish sages, and he asks of God how the sinful nation is going to survive in the heat of the noonday sun. He does not want to be "veiled" (not knowing how they will survive).
    - Verse 8 – These words of the Lord were the response to Moses, but directed at the nation, instructing her to **feed thy kids beside the shepherds' tents**, i.e.: learn from the Law and the Prophets.
    - Verse 9 – This is a reference to the remnant being like the horses of Pharaoh…destined for judgment.
    - Verse 10 – The laws and precepts of the Torah are the harness ropes over the cheeks and the yoke around the neck of the maiden, making her an object of beauty rather than destruction.
    - Verse 11 – The tablets of stone and the 10 Commandments are the borders and studs.
    - Verse 12 – This represents the Law being given; God smells the odor of His people and is reminded of His love for them, thus sending Moses back to the people.

- Verse 13 – Moses is going back to a people deserving punishment and, figuratively, already on the altar of sacrifice, but God will draw them to Himself and tenderly save them.

- Verse 14 – The Ark of the Covenant (the kippur) is given as an instruction immediately after the golden calf.

- Verse 15 – When the children of Israel are obedient, they are beautiful, as the proper sacrifice on the altar.

- Verse 16 – Israel responds and rejoices in a fruitful relationship.

SONG OF SOLOMON 1:1-17

The Maiden Speaks | Song of Solomon 1:1-7

▶ Verse 1 – This is the ninth of 10 songs, according to the Jewish Targum.

▶ Verse 2 –

- Chapter 1 is written from the perspective of the final outcome of the story. That is, it is a foreshadowing of the love-relationship. Later, the story will back track and we will see the love develop.

- The woman (the remnant of Israel) is immediately presented as one desirous of the King's love and the expression of that love. She will be seen to lack the confidence in herself. Her love is going to be much more variable than that of the King. Her "self-esteem" is weak and she often finds fault with herself. This is an allegory of the love of the remnant for her King.

- The **kisses of his mouth** should not be seen as erotic, for the mouth is the only thing we have with which to kiss. This is not "kisses on the mouth" in an erotic sense. Here, the maiden desires public display of affection.

- Verse 3 –
  - **Ointment** - The word is most often translated "oil."
  - An **ointment** in Biblical days was used for anointing. It represented the reign of a priest or king.
  - The **virgins love thee** because He was able to anoint them for leadership in the coming Kingdom.
    - In the last days, there is a bride and also the **virgins** who love the groom.
    - Interpretations abound, and one should always question the assumptions.
    - Whether the **virgins** represent the church, the remnant of the Jewish people, or some other group is a matter of debate.
    - It is not a matter of debate that there is a group represented by **virgins**.
- Verse 4 –
  - Draw me –
    - This is the final desire of the remnant. She passionately wants to be loved by her King. (See Hos. 11:4 and Ps. 45:14.)
    - The Jewish Targum states that the words **Draw me, we will run after thee** were spoken by the righteous in the days of the Exodus when they saw the *shekinah* glory in the pillar of fire and the cloud.
  - **We will be glad** - Notice the 1st person plural. In some manner, the beloved remnant comes with an escort of fair maidens (see v. 3).
  - **We will remember...** -
    - An alternate translation:

- "More than of wine will we tell of your loving, for more than the handsome You do they love."[1]
- In this sense, the maidens say of the King: You are better than the wine and better than all the handsome young men of the Kingdom.

▶ Verse 5 –

- **I am black** - This should be compared to the appearance of the King in Song of Solomon 5:10. Here, the remnant is ashamed of her looks in comparison to that of the King.
    - The Targum, in taking the view that this chapter covers the history of Israel, states that the children of Israel turned black from heat and soot in making the golden calf, but when they repented, their faces began to shine. This occurred when they made curtains for the tabernacle that allowed the *shekinah* to once again dwell among the people.
- Ye daughters of Jerusalem –
    - Throughout the song, these are the other women of the King's harem. Since they must be seen as part of the redeemed, yet not the coming remnant, we will consider them to be the Old Testament saints.
    - The phrase **daughters of Jerusalem** is used seven times in the book, always in a positive manner.
    - The phrase is also used eight times outside of this book, in singular or plural forms. It appears that the singular is a reference to the remnant while the plural is a reference to the Old Testament saints.

---

1 Goulder, Michael D. The Song of Fourteen Songs. Vol. 36. Sheffield: JSOT Press, 1986. Print. Journal for the Study of the Old Testament Supplement Series. [This book is not recommended for a dispensational study of the Song of Solomon].

- The prophets always speak in the singular and always (with the possible exception of Is. 37:22) in reference to the future remnant.
  - In Micah 4:8, it says, "**The kingdom shall come to the daughter of Jerusalem**" (in the singular), and the reference is to the remnant.
  - In Zephaniah 3:14, the daughter rejoices because **the Lord hath taken away thy judgments** (v. 15).
  - In Zechariah 9:9, the daughter is told to rejoice because **thy King cometh unto thee**.
  - In Luke 23:28, on the way to the cross, Jesus instructs the **Daughters of Jerusalem** to **weep not for me, but weep for yourselves, and for your children**.
- **The tents of Kedar** - The tents of Kedar are seen as being *far away from God* (Ps. 120:5) and the **curtains of Solomon** are presumably the curtains of the Temple. Thus, while the comparison is referring to their darkness, the picture is also "both near and far."

▶ Verse 6 –

- This is likely a both literal and figurative: a darkness from the sun and a darkness from sin.
- The Targum view is that this is the address of the Jewish assembly to the nations. They are **black** with sin (not skin color) because **mine own vineyard have I not kept**, but they followed the gods of other nations. Since Israel is held to a higher standard, they are **black** while the other nations are not.

- Verse 7 –

  - **Tell me** – The remnant longs to know where the King will be so that in the heat of the day she can find respite from the sun. She no longer wants to be among **the flocks of thy companions** but rather in the tent of the King.

  - **Why should I be as one that turneth aside** –

    - Another rendering is "why am I as one veiled, By the ranks of thy companions?" (YLT).

    - In either rendering, the remnant desires to be in the fold rather than **as one that turneth aside** or as one "veiled" (either reference to the blinding of the Jewish people or their mourning).

The King Speaks | Song of Solomon 1:8-11

- Verse 8 –

  - The King does not answer her question, but tells her how to find her answer: **by the footsteps of the flock**.

    - That is, "You'll find the King when you follow Israel's own teaching (the Law and the prophets)."

    - It is important to recognize that Israel is going to be brought to salvation by the Hebrew Scriptures (the Old Testament), not the Greek Scriptures (the New Testament).

  - Note: an alternate understanding is that this is the **daughters of Jerusalem** (v. 5) who are singing this portion of the song, toward the young lady, as a means of encouragement.

- Verse 9 – The King continues talking to the maiden. A comparison to **a company of horses** is not flattering, and **horses in Pharaoh's**

chariots is even less flattering. Since Pharaoh is never seen positively in the Bible, it is problematic to make this verse a *positive comparison*. Rather, the Lord is expressing grief over the remnant, that she is (at this point) aligned with that which shall soon be destroyed in the sea.

- Verse 10 - Here, the King describes the beauty of the maiden's cheeks when they are enhanced with **rows of *jewels***, or "garlands" (YLT).

    - The Hebrew word תּוֹרִם [*torim*] means a series or sequence of the same thing, often described as a "braid."
    - The word is used in v. 11 and translated as **borders**.
    - In the KJV, note that *of jewels* is supplied and is not in the text. It is a very plausible interpretation that the King says, "Even though I've compared you to the **horses in Pharaoh's chariots**, I still believe you would be beautiful with a bridle and harness, being brought under control."
    - The Targum teaches that this verse represents the Torah's laws and precepts as the rope and yoke (represented by the **neck with chains of gold**). That is, when the remnant comes into obedience, she is a beautiful thing.

- Verse 11 - The word **borders** is the same Hebrew word as **rows** in v. 10.

    - Since this is in the context discussing the need for a bridle and yoke, the King says He will make these instruments of control a thing of beauty.
    - The Targum views the **borders of gold** to be the two tablets of stone and the **studs of silver** to be the words on the stones (see Ps. 12:6- *The words of the Lord are pure words: as silver...*).

The Maiden Speaks | Song of Solomon 1:12-14

- ▸ Verse 12 –
  - The odor of the remnant (whether pleasant or odorous) comes to the attention of the King.
  - Most Christians would view the smell as pleasant, while the Jewish interpretation is odorous.
  - The Targum teaches that this is representative of the Lord sending Moses off the mountain, having given him the **borders of gold with studs of silver** which are the tablets and their laws. God *smells* the odorous work of His people, as they are making the golden calf.

- ▸ Verse 13 –
  - Though the KJV presents this as words of the maiden toward the King, the grammar does not specify. The YLT is more grammatically accurate: "A bundle of myrrh *is* my beloved to me, Between my breasts it lodgeth."
  - Regardless of the gender, the picture is one of love, tenderness, and sacrifice.
    - If the woman is speaking, then **my wellbeloved** is the bundle of myrrh (representative of a sacrifice) being sacrificed for the remnant.
    - If the King is speaking, then the woman is on the altar of sacrifice, and He is going to rescue her.
  - The Targum teaches that this is reminiscent of Isaac being sacrificed on the altar and spared, which is a picture of the remnant, about to be sacrificed but spared at the last minute.

- Verse 14 - The Hebrew רֹפֶּה [*koper*] is of the same root as *kippur*, the covering, ransom, or pitch. If this speaks of the King, then the ransom is perhaps in view. If it speaks of the maiden, then the beauty of the **camphire**, or henna, is in view.

- Which view? The most likely view of vv. 13-14 is that they are spoken of the King by the maiden. The Jewish interpretation has taken them as spoken by the King describing the maiden. The Jewish interpretation likely came from a desire to avoid the easy comparisons with Jesus.

The King and Maiden Dialogue | Song of Solomon 1:15-17

- Verse 15 - The King praises the maiden for her beauty. In the Targum, the reference is to the beauty of Israel when she is obedient, bringing the sacrifice of a dove.

- Verse 16 - The maiden responds to the love of her King and rejoices in the fruitfulness of the relationship when she is rightly aligned with him.

- Verse 17 - In the Jewish interpretation, this is the interjection of Solomon rejoicing in the Temple, with a forward look to the future and final Temple of "King Messiah." However, since the Hebrew word translated as **house** is plural (and should be "houses"), seeing the Temple in this verse doesn't work. Rather, it could be a celebration of the King that both he and his fiancée are blessed with the safety and wealth of good houses.

SONG OF SOLOMON 2:1-17

The Maiden Speaks | Song of Solomon 2:1-6

- Verse 1 – The Self-description of the Maiden
  - Even though this has most often been associated as a title of the Lord, it is more likely that the bride is speaking. The possible reason that this is associated with Christ is the prevailing mindset that one should look for Christ in every line of the Old Testament.
  - When is a **rose** not a rose? When it is a *crocus*. The word used here is somewhat unknown, but undoubtedly not a rose.
  - **Sharon** is the fertile plane along the coastline on the Mediterranean Sea.
- Verse 2 – An Interjection from the King
  - Here, the King speaks to the maiden, who had compared herself to the **lily**.
  - Both the rose of Sharon and the lily-of-the-valley were very humble flowers.
  - The King seeks to encourage the young lady.

- Verse 3 – The Maiden's Description of Her King
  - Continuing the comparisons with nature, the maiden compares the groom to the **apple tree among the trees** and the blessing of its fruit.
  - Notice that there is a Hebrew word for **apple,** thus the fruit of the tree of knowledge of good an evil was likely not an apple.
- Verse 4 – The Invitation to the **banqueting house**
  - The Hebrew means "the house of wine."
    - The word for wine is used 141 times in the Hebrew Scriptures, and only here is it translated **banqueting house**.
  - The word **banner** is used 14 times in the book of Numbers and is translated as "standard," designating the tribes by their identity.
- Verse 5 – The Maiden's Request
  - According to www.onelook.com, a flagon is "a large metal or pottery vessel with a handle and spout; used to hold alcoholic beverages (usually wine)."
  - However, the Hebrew word is "grape cakes" (or raisin-cakes).
    - It is an unknown term and every ancient and modern writer has struggled with its meaning.
    - Therefore, it is best to say that this was something that would "sustain" the maiden.

The King Speaks | Song of Solomon 2:7-9

- Verse 7 – The Charge
  - The pronoun **you** is inherently in the masculine (See Rth. 1:9), but this is the groom speaking to the **daughters of Jerusalem**.

- A KJV note: **you** is part of an object while "ye" is a subject, as in "ye shall know the truth, and the truth shall make you free" (Jn. 8:32).
- The phrase **"till he please"** would not be correct because the Hebrew is either feminine or neuter.
    - NKJV says, "till it please"
    - Young's Literal says, "till she please."
- Since the maiden represents the remnant of Israel, we see that the groom has a tender love for Israel, but he will not allow her to be disturbed "till she please." Until this time, God protects and sustains her.
- God's work among His people-
    - In Nehemiah, God deals directly with His people who return to Him.
    - In Esther, God deals indirectly with His people who are away from Him.
    - In this passage, God is allowing His people (the bride) to sleep "till she please."
- It is no mistake that, as soon as "she pleases," she hears **the voice of my beloved** and **he cometh.** Compare to the tears of Jesus and His promise of return given in Matthew 23:39.

▶ Verse 8 - How eager is the love of the King, yet he will not allow the maiden to be awakened before she is ready.

▶ Verse 9 - After "she pleases," He comes. And when He comes, He enters Jerusalem and, thus, **standeth behind our wall** and is **shewing himself through the lattice.**

The Maiden Quotes the King | Song of Solomon 2:10-13

- Verse 10 - Compare Matthew 24:30-31.

- Verse 11 - Compare Matthew 24:29-30.

- Verse 12 - In every appearance, this seems to be the beginning of the millennial Kingdom. Compare Isaiah 35:1-2, Hosea 14:5-7, Psalm 40:3,

- Verse 13 - Both the fig and the grape are pictures of Israel.
  - In Luke 13:6-7, the fig tree was cut down. Here, the fig tree is putting forth fruit.
  - Matthew 24:32-34 says that when the fig tree **putteth forth leaves** that "He is near."

The King Speaks | Song of Solomon 2:14

- The King continues to show his delight in the bride, who is hidden in the **secret** *places* **of the stairs**.

- Literally, that would be "the secret place of the ascent" (YLT) or the "secret place of the steep place" (Strong's).

- Remember that in the last days God will prepare a secret place for His people (Ps. 91:1).

The Couple Speaks | Song of Solomon 2:15

- The word **take** is a strong word, as in "capture" or "seize."

- This is either the King or the King and his bride together (note the "**us**").

- **The foxes –**
  - Ezekiel 13:4 compares the false prophets to foxes.
  - In Luke 13:32, King Herod is called a fox by Jesus.
  - This has to be a derogatory phrase, meaning, "Capture the false prophets" (which will be many in the day of the Second Coming).

The Maiden Speaks | Song of Solomon 2:16-17

- Here, and continuing into chapter 3, the bride longs for her King.

SONG OF SOLOMON 3:1-11

The Maiden Speaks | Song of Solomon 3:1-4

- Verse 1- The Nightmare

    - As the maiden speaks, she represents the remnant during the tribulation.

        - **Night** is seen as a time of fear in verse 8 and Isaiah 26:9 (which also speaks of the longing of the soul) as well as in other places in Hebrew Scriptures.

    - **I sought him, but I found him not** - Compare to Hosea 5:5 and John 7:34.

- Verse 2- The Desperate Search

    - In the days of Tribulation, Israel will frantically look for her Messiah.

    - Compare Jeremiah 5:1

- Verse 3-4a - **The Watchmen**

    - Do not confuse this with the two witnesses or the 144,000.

- These **watchmen** are the *guards* of Israel, and they are always seen in a negative light in the Song of Solomon (See Song. 5:7, where the word is used twice).
- Note that the **watchmen** didn't provide any help. After she left them, she found **him**.

▸ Verse 4b – The Visit to the Mother's House

- Compare to Song of Solomon 8:2, where the mother is the one **who would instruct me**.
    ○ This is the remnant introducing the Messiah to all of Israel.
    ○ Hosea 2:5 says that the **mother** who **conceived** the remnant has **played the harlot**.

The King Speaks | Song of Solomon 3:5

▸ See notes on 2:7, an identical verse.

The Narrator Speaks | Song of Solomon 3:6-11

▸ Verse 6 – Who *is* this that commeth?

- This is either a reference to the bride or the **bed, which** *is* **Solomon's.**
- NASB changes **who** to *what*, but the pronoun doesn't merit the change.
- Strong's says the Hebrew word is an "interrogative pronoun of persons" and refers to Strong's Hebrew #4100 which is the pronoun of things.
- The 1890 Darby Bible says, "Who is this, *she* that cometh," making it a reference to the bride.

- In the KJV, it can go either way.
- My personal preference is that verse 6 talks of the bride and verse 7 of the bed.
  - Song of Solomon 8:5 also speaks of **this that cometh up from the wilderness**, and in that verse, it is clearly the bride.
  - Verse 6 is a very feminine description, which is more fitting of the bride (on the other hand, the **pillars of smoke** and the **myrrh and frankincense** could have reference to Jesus Christ).

▶ Verse 7 – The **bed, which *is* Solomon's**
- This is the first time Solomon is revealed as the King, by name, fitting with the prophetic nature of the book in which the bride does not fully know her King until the wedding.

▶ Verses 7-8 - **Threescore valiant men**
- Though many take this to be a positive symbol, it is more likely a negative.
- First, the numbers 6, 60, 600, etc. are always man-based numbers.
- Second, the **valiant of Israel** are men who are **expert in war** and have **fear in the night**. This sounds more like the false shepherds of Israel who are going against the King rather than serving the King.
- If I am correct in this, then this would be the enemies of the remnant who are trying to stop the marriage.
- Concerning **fear in the night**, compare Psalm 91:5.

▶ Verses 9-10 – The **chariot**. The Hebrew word translated **chariot** is only used here in the Hebrew Scriptures. It is a "palanquin" (YLT) (a chair carried by at least four men).

- Verse 11 –

    - The phrase **daughters of Zion** is used 30 times in the Hebrew Scriptures, and would make a valuable study.
    - Compare Zechariah 2:10, 9:9. Also note that Micah 4:8 says that **the kingdom shall come to the daughter of Jerusalem**.
    - Note that in verse 6, the woman is in the **wilderness,** and here, the **daughters of Zion** are instructed to **go forth**. Then, in Micah 4:10, the **daughter of Zion** will **go forth out of the city** and **there shalt thou be delivered; there the Lord shall redeem thee**.

Summary of Chapter 3

In this chapter, we read about the end of the dark night of separation between the Jewish remnant and her King. As the bride finally wakes up (not until she is ready, v. 5), she goes on a frantic search for her King. The guardians of Israel (60 of them) are of no help to her, but she continues to look until she finds Him. Upon finding her King, she takes Him to her mother's house, where she had been educated, and introduces the King to her mother (Israel). In the end, the **daughters of Zion** rejoice.

SONG OF SOLOMON 4:1-5:1

The King Speaks | Song of Solomon 4:1-15

▶ Verse 1 – In chapter 3, the bride and groom are preparing for the wedding. In chapter 4, they are together.

- **Behold, thou *art* fair –**
  - The chapter begins with the groom expressing his delight in the beauty of the bride, using the imagery of the land of Israel.
  - While this is awkward to the western reader, such is natural when one realizes that the *land* shall be called *Beulah* (married).
  - Isaiah 62:1-5 is the necessary background (and the prophetic equivalent) to this chapter.
- **doves' eyes** – These words are almost identical to Song of Solomon 1:15.
- **thy locks** – This is not locks of hair but rather a veil.
- **Thy hair is as a flock of goats –**

- ○ **Gilead** is the land east of the Jordan that was occupied by Gad and Manasseh.
  - ○ A **flock of goats** descending down the mountainside would be a beautiful agricultural scene.
- ▸ Verse 2 - **Thy teeth** –
  - ▪ In a land of sheep and goats, the pictures of verses 1-2 are the most beautiful pictures of sheep and goats.
  - ▪ Here, the sheep are freshly shorn and clean and are seen at the time of producing offspring, each one having born twins with no barrenness among them.
- ▸ Verse 3 –
  - ▪ **Thy temples** –
    - ○ These are **temples** not *cheeks*. There is another Hebrew word for cheek.
    - ○ Some translations (ESV, NRSV, NLT, GNB, *The Message*) change to *cheeks* because the translators cannot understand how **temples** can be referred to as **pomegranate**.
    - ○ Better to allow the words to stand in spite of the translator's inability to comprehend their meaning.
  - ▪ **thy locks** - As in verse 1, this is a veil, not locks of hair. This gives the knowledge to the reader that the marriage has not yet taken place.
- ▸ Verse 4 –
  - ▪ When it is understood that this is a description of the land, which will soon be *Beulah*, these descriptions begin to make more sense. When describing a woman, they are simply odd.

- In the ancient day, it is believed that the **bucklers** and **shields** were hung on citadels after a victory.

▶ Verse 5 – As it has been throughout this description, one must use the wildest of imaginations to try to make comparison to a woman's body. This is a description of the *land* not the *woman*.

▶ Verse 6 –

- **Until the day break…shadows flee away –**
    - At first, this appears to be a contradiction because when the sun rises at day break, shadows will *appear*, not **flee away.**
    - This seems so scientifically undeniable that the NASB, without merit in the text, changed the break of day to the "cool of the day when the shadows flee away."
    - However, when Scripture is allowed to interpret itself, the meaning becomes clear. Jeremiah 6:4 says that when **the day goeth away** that the **shadows of the evening are stretched out**. So, the *frightening* shadows *of the night* will **flee away** when the sun comes out.

- **mountain of myrrh…hill of frankincense –**
    - During the night, the King will be at the **mountain of myrrh** and the **hill of frankincense**.
    - This is either a reference to the time of the absence of Israel's King, where He is associated with His death more than His presence, or it is possibly a reference to the "secret place of the Almighty at which the bride is hidden."
    - While myrrh and frankincense are associated with death and burial in the New Testament, in the Song of Solomon it is associated with beauty and wealth.

- Verse 8 –
  - **Come** –
    - The word **come** is supplied by the translators, despite not being italicized.
    - The spouse is not coming **from Lebanon**, but rather *someone is being invited* to the peaks of Lebanon to look down upon the land.
    - It could even be translated, "With me from Lebanon...my spouse [look at her] with me from Lebanon."
  - *My* **spouse** - This is the first of six times the bride is called the **spouse**.
  - **from the lions' dens...mountains of the leopards** - Lebanon was known as the place of the lions. Now, with the millennium beginning (within the allegory), it is safe to stand (the shadows have fled - v. 6).
- Verse 9 –
  - **ravished** - The root word is "to gain or capture the heart."
  - **my sister, my spouse** - This double term doesn't speak of incest but of the closeness of the relationship.
- Verse 10 – The bride made these same comparisons of the groom in Song of Solomon 1:1-4.
- Verse 11 –
  - The land is producing the *milk and honey* of the millennial promises.
  - **the smell of Lebanon** –
    - As in Hosea 14:5-7 and Isaiah 60:13, Lebanon is presented as the standard of beauty and freshness.

- o Even in modern days, before Hezbollah destroyed Lebanon, it was often considered the "Paris," "pearl," "Riviera," "jewel," and even "Switzerland" of the Middle East.
- ▶ Verse 12 –
  - The words **inclosed** and **shut up** are from the same word in Hebrew.
  - The King is speaking about the protected status of the bride. (In ancient Israel, a walled vineyard and a sealed and protected spring were protected from enemy intrusion.)
- ▶ Verses 13-14 – The *Beulah land* is described in its richest glory.
- ▶ Verse 15 – Compare to Jeremiah 2:13. In both ancient and modern Israel, *living water* was fresh, moving water (as opposed to stagnant and perhaps deadly water).

The Bride Speaks | Song of Solomon 4:16

Here, for the first time in this chapter, the bride speaks, calling upon the gentle winds to stir the pleasant fragrances of her land and inviting the groom into **his garden**. This is the beautiful future awakening of the bride.

The King Speaks | Song of Solomon 5:1

The groom (Jesus Christ) has said He will always accept the invitation of His bride (Israel). Here, the acceptance of the invitation is shown.

Note: Verse 1 belongs with chapter 4, as a response to Song of Solomon 4:16, more than with chapter 5, which thematically begins with 5:2.

SONG OF SOLOMON 5:2-16

The Maiden Speaks | Song of Solomon 5:2-8

▸ Verse 2 –

- Verse 2 is another point within the cycle of the storytelling in which the author goes back to the beginning of the relationship.

- The bride sleeps, but her **heart waketh** at the **voice** of her **beloved that knocketh**. This is reflected in Revelation 3:20, a verse written to the last day's remnant of Israel.

- In keeping with the "land" theme of chapter 4, here the King offers the land the **dew** of the morning. These are meaningless (or awkward) words without the "Jerusalem as bride" concept, but perfectly meaningful when in the light of *Beulah land*.

▸ Verse 3 –

- This is a difficult verse to interpret, but likely the bride is showing reluctance, something that is seen throughout the Song.

- Compare to Revelation 16:15 and Luke 11:7, for example.

- Verse 4 –
    - While this verse is almost exclusively interpreted in a sexual context, the student of the Word will do well to allow Scripture to interpret Scripture.
    - The phrase **put in his hand** is used 8 times in the Hebrew Scriptures.
        - In Exodus 22:7 & 10, the phrase is used for thievery.
        - In Exodus 24:11, it is used as an expression of punishment.
        - In 1 Samuel 26:9, it is used as protection from an enemy.
        - In Job 28:9, it is an expression of God's mighty power on the creation.
        - In Esther 8:7, it is a term of destruction.
        - In 1 Chronicles 13:10, it is a cause of death.
    - The phrase **by the hole** is used 2 other times in the Hebrew Scriptures.
        - In 2 Kings 12:10, it is a hole in the lid of a box.
        - In Ezekiel 8:7, it is a hole in the wall that could be used as a starting place for digging out an opening.
    - The phrase **were moved** is used 3 other times in the Hebrew Scriptures.
        - In Jeremiah 31:20, the Lord says, **"my bowels are troubled"** for Ephraim.
        - In Zechariah 9:15, the phrase is translated **"make a noise"** in reference to the noises that a drunk person might make.
        - In Psalm 46:6, the phrase is translated **"raged,"** in reference to the heathen.

- With three phrases all given as exclusively negative in every other usage, why is this verse taken as positive by so many interpreters?
    - In light of the very plausible interpretation of verse 3 showing the lack of readiness of the bride, it seems best to take this verse as words of disapproval, not sexual satisfaction. They are even likely to be the description of the tribulation and the response of the bride.

- Verse 5 –
    - Myrrh is always seen in a positive light in the Hebrew Scriptures.
    - Here, the bride shows she has prepared herself for her groom as she unlocks the door to let Him in.

- Verse 6 –
    - In my opinion, verse 6 speaks of the bride between the first and second comings.
        - She had her opportunity to welcome her King at Pentecost when her Beloved came knocking.
        - At that time, she was not interested (v. 3) and experienced the judgment of God (v. 4).
        - Now, in verses 5-6, she looks for Him but His presence is not evident (as in the book of Esther, which signifies the same time period).
    - **Withdrawn** –
        - In Jeremiah 31:22, the only other time this Hebrew word is used, it is translated **"go about"** and is about the backslidden nature of Israel.

- In this case, the bride is searching for the King but He is absent.

- **failed** –
  - The Hebrew word means "to go forth" and is only "failed" by interpretation.
  - Literally it means, "My soul went forth when he spake" (YLT).
  - However, with the context of the words **when he spake**, in reference to verses 2-3, here the bride laments that when she had opportunity, she didn't take it.

▶ Verse 7 –

- The identity of the **watchmen that went about the city** is not revealed, but they are possibly the world leaders in the *age of the Gentiles*.

- They are mentioned in Song of Solomon 3:3, and after she leaves them, she discovers **him whom my soul loveth**.

- Note: the word **watchmen** and **keepers** is the same Hebrew word, יָרְמֹשׁ [*shomer*], "to guard or keep."

The Daughters of Jerusalem Ask a Question & Get an Answer | Song of Solomon 5:9-16

▶ Verse 9 – Here, the **daughters of Jerusalem** answer the bride and are not as thrilled about her **beloved** as she is.

▶ Verse 10 –

- **white and ruddy** - In actuality, **white and ruddy** is a contradiction, since **ruddy** is red or reddish brown. The Hebrew adjective translated **white** means "dazzling, glowing, clear, bright" (Strong's). Young's Literal says, "clear and ruddy."

- **The chiefest** - Because the word translated **chiefest** relates to the *standard* raised above the army (as the word is used in Song. 6:4 and 6:10), this could be translated as the **chiefest** *banner* **among ten thousand**.

- Verses 10-16 - The description of the woman in chapter 4 was as if the King was describing land. Here, the description is as if the bride is describing royalty.

SONG OF SOLOMON 6:1-13

In the previous chapter, the maiden (Israel) was longing for her absent King (Messiah), recognizing too late that she already had her opportunity to be with Him (v. 2), yet rejected it (v. 3), and was now suffering His absence (vv. 4-16).

The Daughters of Jerusalem Speak | Song of Solomon 6:1

- In verse 1, the **daughters of Jerusalem** speak to the bride. This is the sixth time we have seen them within this book.

- Since the daughters represent the ten virgins (Matt. 25), both faithful and unfaithful, here they are speaking to the bride (the all-encompassing land of Israel) saying, "Where is your Messiah?" It is a question of inquiry and of doubt.

- Premise: The *bride* is the *land of Israel*, the *daughters* are the *Jewish people*.

- Premise: the **daughter of Jerusalem** (or Zion) is the land of Israel (or the "collective whole") and is the bride of the Messiah. The **daughters of Jerusalem** (or Zion) are the people of Israel (i.e.: the Jews).

- The term is used eight times outside of the Song of Solomon, all in the singular except one.
  - 2 Kings 19:21 and Isaiah 37:22 are parallel and refer to the city of Jerusalem, though the speech is *anthropomorphic*. (Note the context in 2 Kings 19:32-34.)
  - In Lamentations 2:13 & 15, the **daughter of Jerusalem** is mocked because she has been destroyed, so that **thy breach** *is* **great like the sea** (v. 13).
  - In Micah 4:8, the **daughter** inherits **the kingdom** of God.
  - In Zephaniah 3:14, the **daughter** is instructed to **be glad and rejoice** because her **judgments** and her **enemy** has been removed (Zeph. 3:15); she is referred to as **Jerusalem** in verse 16.
  - In Zechariah 9:9, the daughter is instructed to **rejoice greatly** and to **shout** because **thy king cometh unto thee**.
  - In Luke 23:28, on his way to the crucifixion, Jesus weeps for the **daughters** and warns of their coming destruction. This is the only use of the plural outside Song of Solomon.
- The term is used seven times in the Song of Solomon, all in the plural.
  - In Song of Solomon 1:5, the bride speaks to the **daughters**, and she laments her condition.
  - In Song of Solomon 2:7 and 3:5, the groom speaks to the **daughters**, instructing them not to awaken the bride.
  - In Song of Solomon 3:10, the **chariot** of the bridegroom is **paved** *with* **love** either "by" or "**for**" the **daughters**.
  - In Song of Solomon 5:8, the **daughters** are not as thrilled for the groom as the bride is.

- In Song of Solomon 5:16, the **daughters** hear from the bride how lovely the groom is.
- The term **daughter(s) of Zion** is used 30 times in the Bible.
  - Four times in the plural:
    - Song of Solomon 3:11, equivalent with **daughters of Jerusalem**.
    - Isaiah 3:16-17, referring to the people of Judah who will undergo tribulation.
    - Isaiah 4:4, they shall have their filth washed away.
  - Twenty-six times in the singular:
    - The term is often used in repetition with **daughter of Jerusalem**.
      - ✓ Isaiah 19:21, 37:22; Song of Solomon 3:11; Zechariah 9:9; Zephaniah 3:14
    - In the following passages, the term is clearly a *physical location*.
      - ✓ Psalm 19:14
      - ✓ Isaiah 1:8, 10:32, 16:1, 52:2, 62:11
      - ✓ Jeremiah 4:31 (in context), 6:23
      - ✓ Jeremiah 6:2 – where it is also said that God has considered Jerusalem **a comely and delicate *woman*.**
      - ✓ In Lamentations, the term is used eight times, always as a term for Jerusalem.
      - ✓ Micah 1:13; 4:8,10,13 all use the term in reference to Jerusalem or Zion.

> ✓ Zechariah 2:10 says that the Messiah **will dwell in the midst of thee**.

- Conclusions:
  - The daughters are clearly *not the bride*.
  - The daughters are clearly Jewish.
  - The daughters are equivalent to the 10 virgins of Matthew 25:1-13; some are foolish and some wise, but none of them are the bride.
  - The phrase **daughter of Jerusalem** is never used in Song of Solomon because she is one of two main characters, the bride.
  - The Old and New Testaments are consistent: the Bride of the Messiah (Lamb) is the *Beulah Land* of Israel, which is an all-encompassing term inclusive of the entire Abrahamic Covenant of land, nation, and descendants.

The Bride Responds | Song of Solomon 6:2-3

- Verse 2 - The King's garden was previously mentioned in Song of Solomon 4:12, 15, 16 and 5:1. We must use these passages to interpret the garden. In each of the previous uses, the garden is the land of Israel. Therefore, the cycle of the Song is evident again. Here, the love of the bride and the Groom is in full harmony.
- The cycle (with the current cycle passages noted):
  - Love expressed – Song of Solomon 5:2
  - Love doubted – Song of Solomon 5:3
  - Love distressed – Song of Solomon 5:4-6:1
  - Love completed – Song of Solomon 6:2-12

- While this cycle is general in nature, it is repeated throughout the book.
- Verse 3 - The bride rejoices in the union of bride and Groom.
- **The King Expresses Love | Song of Solomon 6:4-13**
- Verse 4 –
  - **Tirzah** - The Bible records an otherwise unknown woman named **Tirzah**, a kingdom conquered by Joshua named **Tirzah**, and what would be a future capital of the northern kingdom of Israel. However, the Bible never mentions its beauty. It is perhaps better to translate the word, which would be "favorable," making the phrase read, "**Thou *art* beautiful, O my love**, favorable, **comely**...."
  - **comely as Jerusalem** - The comparative **as** is assumed, not required. Therefore, "beautiful Jerusalem" would be an accurate translation.
  - **terrible as *an army*...** - Young's Literal: "Awe-inspiring as bannered hosts."
- Verses 5-7 –
  - **Turn away thine eyes...** - An expression of being overwhelmed by the beauty of the bride.
  - **thy hair...** - A repetition of the remarks of Song of Solomon 4:1-2 and a description of the beauty of the *Beulah Land*.
- Verse 9 –
  - **undefiled** - The Hebrew word is one of "complete," and is translated "coupled" in Exodus 26:34 and 36:29, with the idea that "both halves" are present.

- ***but* one** - In comparison with the many queens, concubines, and virgins, there is but one bride and one land of Israel. One refers to her quantity and her uniqueness. There is only one Israel, and no other.

▶ Verse 11 –

- The entrance of the King into the **garden** is always a reference to the Second Coming.
- **fruits of the valley** – Translated as **greenness** in Job 8:12. YLT translates as "buds," and NASB as "blossoms." The word is used of fresh, promising growth.

▶ Verse 12 –

- That is, "My soul was so eager to go down to the garden that I set upon this task like the chariots of my noble people." Alternately, **Ammi-nadib** could be the name of an unknown person.
- **Ammi-nadib** –
  - **Ammi** is a Hebrew transliteration, meaning "my people."
  - **nadib** is a Hebrew transliteration, meaning "willing." The word *nadib* is used in Song of Solomon 7:1 and is translated "**prince**."

▶ Verse 13 –

- It is not known if this is the word of the King (with the "royal" **we**) or if this is a chorus sung from the *daughters of Jerusalem*. Either way, there is the desire to gaze upon the bride. Note the parallel with Song of Solomon 6:1.
- **Shulamite** - The Hebrew word is תיֹּמַלוּשׁ [shulamit]. The masculine version of the word is המֹלְשׁ [sheloma], and both come from the root שׁלם. The **Shulamite** is nothing more than the *prized wife of Solomon, the King*.

SONG OF SOLOMON 6:13-7:13

The King's Question and Answer | Song of Solomon 6:13-7:9

▶ Verse 13 –

- **What will ye see…?** - This phrase belongs with Song of Solomon 7:1 (as in the Hebrew). The King asks the virgins, **What will ye see in the Shulamite?** He then proceeds to answer the question.

- **the company of two armies** –
    - This phrase begins to answer the previous question.
    - Young's literal places this phrase in Song of Solomon 7:1 and gives the best translation: "As the chorus of 'Mahanaim'." The Mahanaim is simply the soldiers camped at base.
    - It would be best to put this phrase together with **How beautiful are thy feet with shoes** (see note on Song. 7:1).

- For a modern picture of "the chorus of Mahanaim" see https://www.youtube.com/watch?v=JkWGUkQf3e8

▶ Verse 1 –

- **thy feet with shoes** - Likely an allegorical reference to readiness. See Ephesians 6:15 for a comparison.

- **O prince's daughter** - If Israel (Jacob) is the prince, then the bride is the **prince's daughter**.
- **The joints of thy thighs...** - Possibly a reference to Jacob's experience with God in Genesis 32, where the joint of his thigh was dislocated, and thus, the thigh became "sacred" to the nation.
- **a cunning workman** - The work here is spoken of the **joints of thy thighs**, which are the **work...of a cunning workman**. In this case, God Himself is the Workman, and the work He did was done at the Jabbok brook.
- This entire phrase (Song. 6:13b-7:1) fits well with Jacob's experience with God in Genesis 32. In Genesis 32:1-2, Jacob met with the **angels of God** and recognized them as **God's host** (army) and called the place **Mahanaim** (i.e.: the camp of God's hosts). In Genesis 32:7, Jacob divided his own people into **two bands** תוֹנָחַמ [mahanot - feminine plural]. In verse 10, he lamented that **now I am become two bands** and prayed for deliverance in verse 11, claiming the promises to Abraham (v. 12). Jacob sent gifts in advance and then met God at the Jabbok brook, wrestling with him until the break of day, when God **touched the hollow of his thigh; and the hollow of Jacob's thigh was out of joint** (v. 25). At this point, God changes Jacob's name to Israel, saying, **as a prince hast thou power with God and with men (v. 28)**. The root of the word Israel is likely *shar*, meaning "prince." From this point, Israel **halted upon his thigh**, and **the children of Israel eat not of the sinew...which is upon the hollow of the thigh** (vv. 31-32).

▶ Verse 2 –

- **Thy navel...liquor** –
    - As the King proceeds to describe the bride, he uses physical metaphors but is describing *land*, not a woman.

- - Here, he describes the **navel** as a **round goblet** filled with **liquor** or, more accurately, *mixed wine*.
  - **Thy belly…** - Note the interesting comparison with Ruth 3:7, where Boaz (the Kinsman Redeemer / groom) has drunk his wine and then lays down at the grain heap.
- Verse 3 - As in Song of Solomon 4:5, there is no real explanation of such a comparison unless you realize that this is a description of *land and* not *woman*.
- Verse 4 –
  - **Thy neck…** - See Song of Solomon 4:4
  - **Heshbon** and **Bath-rabbim** - **Heshbon** was a city, and **Bath-Rabbim** were "Daughters of Rabbah." Both Heshbon and Rabbah were in the land of Gad, which will someday be part of the completed *beulah land* and which was part of Israel under Solomon's reign. Compare to 2 Samuel 12:26-27.
  - **Thy nose** - This is, presumably, part of Israel under Solomon's reign. See 1 Kings 9:19.
- Verse 7:5 –
  - **Carmel** - **Carmel** is the mountain range upon which Elijah would later challenge the prophets of Baal. In Solomon's day, it was "the vineyard of God" (literal translation of לְכַרְמֶל [karmel, from *karem el*]
  - **And the hair** - Since the **head** is compared to **Carmel**, the **hair of thine head** must be a further description of **Carmel**. In Song of Solomon 4:1, the hair was **as a flock of goats, that appear from mount Gilead,** which is treeless. But Carmel is one of the few natural forests in Israel, and the natural pine trees of the mountain can give it a "purple mountain majesty" look that is similar to the Rocky Mountains.

- **The king *is* held…** - The meaning is not certain, but could be translated, "The King is captivated by your streams." Compare Genesis 30:38 where the word used for **galleries** is translated **gutters**. As before, this description is odd (at best) if describing a woman, but perfectly reasonable when describing land.

▶ Verse 7:9 –

- **my beloved, that goeth down…** - Though many translations and translators make this phrase a statement of the Bride, the Hebrew favors the statement as a continuation of verse 9a, thus, "like the best wine for my beloved, wine that goeth down sweetly…"

- **Causing the lips…to speak** - That is, "causing to speak" (Strong's). Or possibly, "gliding over the lips…" The meaning appears to be, "you are like a great wine that demands the lips of those who taste it to speak."

- **those that are asleep** - Possible interpretation: God will someday so bless the land of Israel that the sleeping people of Israel will wake up and praise Him. In Song of Solomon 5:1, it is the bride that is sleeping.

The Bride's Response | Song of Solomon 7:10-13

▶ Verse 7:10 –

- **I *am* my beloved's** - These are the words of sleeping Israel, awakened in verse 9. They testify of the future relationship of the Jewish land to her God. The words are a repeat of the Bride's celebration in Song of Solomon 2:6 and 6:3.

- **his desire *is* toward me** - Every Christian should remember that God's desire is toward Israel-the land and the people.

- Verses 7:11-12 - Here the bride (the land) responds by saying, "Come to me," and "me" is **the field, the villages, and the vineyards.**

- Verse 7:13 –

  - **Mandrakes** have been associated with fertility since at least the days of Rachel & Leah (Gen. 30:14ff).

  - The picture of this verse is the fruitfulness of the land, and the fruit being **New and old** is a picture of the bounty of the land after the marriage, in the Millennium.

SONG OF SOLOMON 8:1-14

The Bride's Response | Song of Solomon 8:1-3

- This section continues from Song of Solomon 7:10-13

- Verse 1 – **that thou *wert* as my brother** - As the bride continues, she steps back into "reality" in current time, wishing that the marriage had already taken place, that the millennium had arrived. Instead, she is separated from the one she loves. She wishes her beloved was **as my brother** so that they could be affectionate in public.

- Verse 2 – **into my mother's house** -

  - The land (the bride) wants to bring the King (the Messiah) to **my mother's house**, that is, the land longs to introduce the Messiah to Judaism, and Judaism itself (the mother) would give instruction.

  - In the end, it is Judaism that will lead Israel to the Messiah, just as Naomi led Ruth to the Kinsman Redeemer.

The King Speaks to the Daughters of Jerusalem, and They Respond | Song of Solomon 8:4-5a

- Verse 4 - This repeated chorus throughout the book is spoken by the King about the bride. The KJV consistently mistranslates "she" to "he" in these verses.

- Verse 5a – **who *is* this…leaning on her beloved** - The daughters of Jerusalem begin to speak, and repeat a phrase from 3:6, asking who comes **from the wilderness,** as a reference to the bride. This time she comes **leaning upon her beloved,** a sign of the progress of the relationship.

The Bride Speaks | Song of Solomon 8:5b-7

- Verse 5b –
  - Because the pronouns change from third person singular (**her beloved**) to second person masculine (**thee…thy**), we must recognize a change of speakers and subject.
    - Possible speakers are the bride (as in NASB) or the daughters of Jerusalem (though the singular "I" is problematic, unless the daughters speak collectively).
    - The least problematic is to see verse 4 as words of the groom, verse 5a as words of the **daughters of Jerusalem,** and verses 5b-7 as words of the bride.
    - One commentary says:
      - *"Though the divisions between the sections are easy to see, we have problems identifying who the speakers are and how the subsections are related—if at all. Verse 5 in particular is extremely unclear; we do not know*

who is speaking and how exactly the verse relates to what follows."[2]

- **I raised thee up** - **raised** is "awoke," not to be confused with raising a child.
- **under the apple tree** - The **apple tree** is mentioned 4 times in Song of Solomon, all of them positive (6 times in the Old Testament, also positive). There is almost certainly some deeper symbolism, but its meaning is not apparent.
- **thy mother** - There are two times in the Song when the mother of the King is mentioned, here and 3:11. In 3:11, the mother of the King is the nation of Israel, and must be seen so here as well.

▶ Verse 6 –

- **Set me as a seal...** - Here the bride (Israel, the land) wants to be a **seal** upon the **heart** and **arm** of the King (Messiah). The seal is an engraving (as in a signet ring) and, in modern terminology, might best be understood as a tatoo on the heart and arm of the Messiah. This is a plea for eternal love, which cannot be broken, given by the bride.
- **for love *is* strong as death** - The bride has clearly fallen in love with her King!

The Daughters of Jerusalem Speak | Song of Solomon 8:8-9

▶ Here, presumably, the daughters of Jerusalem speak. Since the daughters represent the Jewish people (not the Bride), who is the **little sister** of the Jewish people?

---

[2] Ogden, Graham S., and Lynell Zogbo. *A Handbook on the Song of Songs*. New York: United Bible Societies, 1998. Print. UBS Handbook Series.

- Most commentaries say that the **little sister** is the gentile church, who **hath no breasts** (i.e.: not yet of marriageable age).
  - However, these same commentaries mostly say that the gentile church is the bride, so their commentary is not consistent.
  - Furthermore, the cardinal rule of "Scripture interprets Scripture" is ignored, since no passage compares the gentile church as a sister to the Jewish nation.
- To come to a better understanding of the sister…
  - First, note that the Jewish people are coming to the aid of the **little sister** and will cover her deficiencies in whatever manner is necessary.
  - Second, note that the only reference in the Bible to a "little sister" for the Jewish people is found in Ezekiel 16:46-63, where the older sister is Samaria and the younger sister is Sodom. Ezekiel chides Judah for receiving and protecting her sisters and says they will someday be ashamed for receiving her sisters.
  - So, the younger sister is actually not the church but the pagan "sister" of the Jewish people who cannot be married to the King, yet is unwisely protected and honored among the Jews.

The Bride Speaks | Song of Solomon 8:10-12

▶ Verse 10 - The bride speaks, rejoicing that she **found favour** with the King.

▶ Verse 11 –

- **Solomon had a vineyard...** - **Baal-hamon** is an unknown place and may actually be an allusion to Jerusalem.
  - The name **Baal-hamon** means "father/husband/owner of a tumultuous multitude" and is from the same root as the name Abraham.
  - Since a **vineyard** is often a Biblical allusion to Israel, this could be a reference to Jerusalem itself.
- **He let out the vineyard...** - Speaking prophetically, the King (represented here by Solomon) would **let out the vineyard unto keepers**. The parable of the talents (Matt 25:14-23) is similar.

▶ Verse 12 –

- At the beginning of the Song, the bride laments that she has taken care of everyone else's vineyard, but not her own.
- Here, she says, **my vineyard, which** *is* **mine** (emphasizing her ownership) has been cared for by the King Himself, and thus the **thousand** *pieces* **of silver** (v. 11) belong to Solomon.
- She also gives a blessing to **those that keep the fruit thereof**.
- Could this be a reminder that "I will bless those that bless thee"?

The Final Dialogue Between King and Bride | Song of Solomon 8:13-14

▶ Verse 13 –The King is waiting for the call of His bride. He has repeatedly asked that no one wake her up before her time. Now, He longs for her voice (as He did in Song of Solomon 2:14). Compare Matthew 23:39.

▶ Verse 14 - The bride responds with those blessed and long-sought words: **Make haste, my beloved.** And her King shall appear!

Dispensational Publishing House is striving to become the go-to source for Bible-based materials from the dispensational perspective.

Our goal is to provide high-quality doctrinal and worldview resources that make dispensational theology accessible to people at all levels of understanding.

Visit our blog regularly to read informative articles from both known and new writers.

And please let us know how we can better serve you.

Dispensational Publishing House, Inc.
PO Box 3181
Taos, NM 87571

Call us toll free 844-321-4202

www.DispensationalPublishing.com

www.ingramcontent.com/pod-product-compliance
Lightning Source LLC
Chambersburg PA
CBHW052105110526
44591CB00013B/2359